T0354975

AXCESS

UNIQUE DAVIS

authorHOUSE

AuthorHouse™
1663 Liberty Drive
Bloomington, IN 47403
www.authorhouse.com
Phone: 833-262-8899

Published by AuthorHouse 11/30/2020

ISBN: 978-1-6655-0842-1 (sc)
ISBN: 978-1-6655-0841-4 (e)

Library of Congress Control Number: 2020923390

Print information available on the last page.

Scripture taken from the King James Version of the Bible.

DEDICATED TO GOD, MICHAEL SANDERS, DENNIS HILLIARD JR., & BISHOP TOMMIE A. MURPHY I THANK YOU MEN FOR ALWAYS BEING YOU TO ME FOR THE ACTIONS AND WORDS AND MY SON.

TO MY MOMMY I LOVE YOU, EVERYTHING YOU INVESTED IN ME AND THE EFFORTS OF YOUR LIFE WILL NEVER BE FORSAKEN ONLY LIVE THROUGH ME.

CONTENTS

CHAPTER 1
YOU'VE GOT IT

"YOU'VE GOT IT... SURE. YES YOU DO ", said my mother. "Always remember that you are a winner."

"Yes ma'am", I replied. As I've gotten older, I've allowed those words to replay. Challenges, trials, tribulations arose, and the little voice said *'you've got it, you are winner '*. These words became crucial to a new dimension that was to give me full access.

Let's play a game. I want you to take a moment and recall a few thoughts that come to mind, when you encounter difficulties. Are those thoughts of fear or defeat? What words are you speaking to yourself? Take a piece of paper and write down five (5) things you would say to answer each question. Choose A or B.

<u>Category A</u>	<u>Category B</u>
I can't do it	**I can**
It's too hard	**I'm a conqueror**
My life is horrible	**I'm a survivor**
Nothing good ever happens for me	**I'm a winner**
I'm a loser	**I'll never quit**
I suck	**I'm a fighter**
I'm never gonna be anything	**I will succeed**
I'm a failure	**Nothing can stop me**

Look at your paper. Do you see some of the words that are listed in category A or B?

Category A is words that create and show signs of defeat. Category B is words that create and show signs of words that create and show signs of victory. Now after evaluating what category you are choosing when difficulties occur. Is it category A or category B? You are probably wondering how do my thoughts matter or how I speak to myself relate to when trials occur. Well I am here to tell you what you speak does matter. Not ten percent, twenty percent, or eighty percent it matters a one hundred percent the way you speak and the thoughts you create especially the voices to yourself. Hopefully the words and thoughts you share are from the choices in category A. If not, the words spoken in this book will guide you showing you the new way to gain control through word choice. It is very important to understand that the power of life and death is in the tongue. What you say and feel will come to pass because you begin to subconsciously believe the words and thoughts you are expressing. Once your subconscious mind is activated with the words you choose it becomes your reality. My next question for you what is the true reality you want to create for yourself? Is it the reality of happiness or brokenness; bitterness or joyfulness; hopefulness or fruitfulness. Who does your reality consist of? Is it family, friends and coworkers? Or is it strangers or businesspeople? Who and what do you choose for your reality? These questions are the start to what your reality will consists of. It's so important to understand the first step to living the life you have access to is knowing what, who, when, where and how. Knowing how you want to live out your full desire to create your reality. Knowing who the people that are required to be in your life to create the reality you choose. Once you have created the reality you want mentally. The next step is writing it down. It is so valuable to understand how your thoughts shape your reality. Writing down what you want and creating a plan then executing that plan. It leads to results from the actions you created and completed. As you now have insight to why shifting words in your vocabulary to be in favor of the reality you choose to live and writing down your plan to. Create and execute your hand-picked reality. You could possibly have had a light bulb pop in your head *'I get it, I am ready'*... awesome! I am excited for those light bulbs that when clicked let us elaborate more to have a true understanding.

When you sit down, close your eyes think about the past five years of your life. In what way are you envisioning it? What situations occurred financially, emotionally, physically, arose unexpectedly. Which ones were those that had a great amount of impact on your circumstances; negative or positive? In what ways did you handle situations to create the best outcome? Do you see a way that same situations could had room for reconstructed improvement; possibly prevented or with proper planning propelled to reconstruct the circumstantial outcome. As you recall those past situations when you experienced a negative vs positive outcome what was the thoughts and actions leading up to that moment. Between your subconscious and conscious thoughts did you see a different pattern, or did you experience the same thought process leading up to that moment for each different outcome.

Now let us backtrack to our word choice from Category A and Category B. The words and thoughts both subconsciously and consciously shape the outcome of your circumstances. Are you able to see the correlation between the outcome and the thoughts and words you chose? It was so powerful. My son Michael and I were walking. I began to jog a little and hold his hand because we were rushing, on the way to the take him to school. As I grabbed his hand and pulled him I said, "You're being slow, let's go."

"I'm a slow pokey ", He replied. And I immediately said

"No you're not! Don't let anyone tell you otherwise. You're a fast pokey." Immediately he began to say,

"I'm a fast pokey "excited, speeding up his pace… enthused and repeatedly saying, "Fast pokey, mommy. I'm not a slow pokey, I'm fast pokey"

"Yes, son you are fast. Never let anyone tell you different. You are fast like a Catboy." I encouraged him. A smile spread across his face. Those words gave him endurance; hope again. He became a champ, even though before he thought he was a slow poke.

Parenting 101… I have no idea where the vocabulary of 'slow pokey' arose from, but I do know that it didn't come from me. I never spoke those words to my son Michael. What that teaches us is to be careful about the words you speak to our children. Also, be careful about how you allow others to speak to your child. Now if we relate this to our now, are you able to identify the words you spoke or allowed someone to speak to you that created your reality up until today. So many words so many thoughts you have about who you are and what you call yourself to be and about where you are. Your thoughts and words matter 100% of the time, starting right now. Tell yourself, *"(Your Name) is victorious and conqueror over all things. I have complete access."* Awesome! Look at your posture as you repeat that sentence. Stand with your back straight, head high, and shoulders back with chest out. You are awakening your subconscious mind to have thoughts to match your conscious mind. How do you feel? Did those words allow you to see a different reality than the one you currently live? Do you see improved results in your reality? The words and thoughts make up your reality 100%. Writing down the plan that creates your reality is the steppingstone to seeing what needs to be done and knowing what reality you choose to create for yourself. It will allow you to manifest every detail of your life. In response you would say some things. *'I can't control what happens throughout my life... My tire goes flat. A car accident caused traffic.'*... Of course I get it, you are absolutely correct. You cannot control it, but you have the control over every detail, especially the way you speak to yourself.

Once you have written down every special detail that you choose to create your reality with; the time, the places, the where's and what's. You've got it, it is yours all yours. You are a conqueror of your life; the good, the bad, the ups and downs. Plan your reality the way you want to see it go. Visualize it in your mind and soul... your plan. Read it aloud to yourself daily take the actions needed for each plan you have written out for the reality you choose to create. You've got it! You will create. You will plan. You will write. You will speak life into your plan by choosing the words that will bring power and purpose to you completing and executing your plan. It will bring you joy to speak life into you reality, because you are handcrafting your life. You know that regardless of the circumstances the plan of the reality you choose is much greater than circumstances or situations occurring on the way there. You will know now that because every word or thought that you speak matters. You will choose those words and thoughts of victory, not defeat. You will choose the words of life, not death. You will choose the words of light not dark; the words of beauty, not horror. You will empower yourself with word choices that are optimistic, not pessimistic.

Your thoughts, no matter what you write down or plan, will sink or blossom purely based on focus. You can think your way to the opposite reality of your choice. Don't believe me; ask some doctors who have had patients whose thoughts caused them to have diseases that were totally stress-related. Some of these patients actually died from diseases and complication that started as a thought. If you have not noticed, words and thoughts matter 100% of the time has been mentioned numerous times. Before going further into creating your reality or enjoying life to its fullest potential, is to know that you will not get the results you need and it will be 100% harder to go through without the right words and thoughts which excites the mindset. You've got it. Do not look at yourself and say what you cannot do. Look at what you are saying, what you can do, will do, and know that you are going to do. This is the plan you have, and the results will come. The results will come because you created a plan, you manifest the plan, you took massive action, you spoke life into situations through choosing words that accelerate. Once you start writing your plan, do not let it go. Set a goal and go for it, do not talk yourself out of it by having negatives thoughts of defeat. Sometimes we are unaware that our subconscious thoughts are controlling our life. It's the mind inside the mind telling the mind what you really feel. It is where the fear is located that causes doubt. Talk to yourself. Tell yourself each situation is victorious. Tell everything in your life you have access to be the best. Stay focused on the reality you want and nothing you do not want. Choose the reality that allows you to be the best version of you. Create your reality. Plan your reality. You don't have to reason with what you want in life. Rewrite your plan. Tell yourself you can do it. Execute it so you can live the hand-picked life you create. That means if you start, when you line a plan up, that plan will work out. No one will know what your plan is. Only you know because you wrote it out. Take your time. Believe in yourself. Know that you are worthy of all of your desires, goals and life assets. A little secret, no one else or no certain thing matters when it comes to your life process. Only you can get in the way of your own reality and thoughts. Sometimes we are our own worst critics and enemies. The only story and reality we should experience is one hundred percent of what we create. Every reaction and action in our life we have control over. You have the power to live out the reality you created, continuously talking control over your thoughts; changing your words to benefit the reality of your creation.

Write down your plan. Shape your thoughts to receive the greatest outcome and live the hand-picked life you created.

As you do know, life has it's share of unknown turns. Unfortunately, we allow unexpected twists and events play major roles in how we assist ourselves in choosing what actions to accept and thoughts to create. But now we're able to have life occurrences and create words and thoughts of life by the use of purposeful words. Understanding that you have access for greatness no matter what life throws at you. Of course, some days, planned days are more difficult to endure than others; but if you have faith you can keep going. You have complete access through God. It will be no battle too big, no plan too big for God.

CHAPTER 2
KEEP GOING

TRUTH OF THE MATTER IS, NO matter what you see with the natural eye, God gave you complete access for every area of your life; to fulfill any dream or reality you have. *Faith is the substance of what is not seen.* Once you have your reality written down on your paper and you have planned your goals, even when the unfortunate happens, you know you have complete access through faith and God's favor. Let us be honest, it is easier to *say* what we can do than to do it when we are in that exact moment of life when you have to endure and practice what we preach. It looks like, as long as you do it once you do have the power to overcome those challenges. It will always become what your thoughts lead it to be.

In chapter one I strongly advised and gave examples on the words needed to speak life and the way to change your thoughts to create and execute your hand-picked reality. In most cases, as human beings, it is unbelievably hard to do that; which could lead to destruction of dreams, aspirations, goals and faith. I love the lyrics to a song I sung, at the age of 6 in my afterschool program, by Donnie McClurkin, **<u>Yes You Can</u>** ". The lyrics are as follow:

> " yes you can, you can do anything if you try, just try yes you can but you have to believe and rely on what you have inside. No matter what if you can just conceive it if you believe it then you can achieve it. For God gave the provision made the decision. Yea you can do all things through your faith "

The words of the song, eighteen plus years later, still has a major, empowering role in my life. Anytime I sense detours or that unfortunate event arises I replay these words and I start to tell myself that I can do anything. The words you use to get over the hump will keep you going through to next trial and as long as you do it once you do have the power to do it again… and again. Hold on to that power God gives through Him, which is called ***access***. You are archeries of your words. You create your life by what comes out of your mouth. Remember, the time you were excited and had everything aligned to go the way you planned in your head, then boom; the unexpected came, a twist you were not ready for. What was the next move to have you doubting or having total control and faith over what is to come next? Remember the time when you had doubt that the plan you had would fail when that unfortunate twist came about. did your plan still work out or did it go exactly the way you doubted it to go ? can you recall the time when you had faith during the time an unfortunate twist came about in the plans you had. Did your plan still workout and if it did not at that exact moment later down the road did it work for your benefit or did you realize why it did not go as you planned? I ask you these questions so you can now see and assess the way you go about handling unexpected twist that were not planned in your life while achieving and knocking out your goals and accomplishments. I am going to break down why it is important to always have faith when things come unexpectedly/ when you always have faith you give nothing else power to take your happiness or joy no matter the circumstances. If you have faith as a mustard seed, it can move mountains. Faith can only give outcomes, hope and prosperity; even when your circumstances tell you it is not going to work. By you having faith, you know absolutely for sure it will work in your favor. That gives you control and full access over how you handle the unexpected events that arise. Faith gives you the ability to, most of all, keep going forward; seeing the best results for the outcome without the now. God gives us complete access to complete our destiny and dreams that he placed in us through Him. According to His word he gave us access to do all things; to know ***all things will work together for your good***. It is in His plan for us through Him. This brings deeper understanding on why faith and trusting God in all aspect of our life but more importantly trusting when adversities come our way. When the plans, that we have, take unexpected twists or do not work out the way we desire; God wants to see our desires come to pass. But do you have the ability to be strong and endure the road until you get the reality you hand- picked. I do not agree that it will be easy or microwave, but I do believe that having a continuous positive outlook will make the journey easier.

When adversity comes and detours our plans, as humans we begin to display and experience a range emotions; anger, bitterness, defeat, unworthiness and shame, realizing God removed us from the real adversity and wants to promote us to our own vision of plans. Trust his ways they are bigger and far greater than ours. Imagine if Netflix, after the plan of becoming partners with Blockbuster, gave up and doubted their vision because Blockbuster said, *'NO'* to merging. Now look on every television and ask yourself, where is Blockbuster today? Let me help you, they are completely alone. Most importantly Netflix arose, wiping all Blockbusters out of business and still carried out their vision; becoming a record- charting billion-dollar company. If you asked yourself what would be more beneficial for business… to become partners having profits or owning all equity. The owner Reed Heedings was expecting a different outcome with blockbuster, which if they did not keep going, enduring the journey after their adversity it would not have become the company that we know today called Netflix; streaming shows and entertainment. Another successful owner, Mark Zuckerberg of Facebook, faced challenges in his plan when he invited five of his closet peers to his dorm room expecting them to be on board with creating a social platform for the internet. That day more than ten years ago three of those walked out the dorm going back to class calling his idea not possible, crazy etc. Two of his peers stayed and believed in the vision; now profiting millions as co-founders. If Facebook founder Mark Zuckerberg focused on how his plan didn't go the way he envisioned in the beginning, and didn't keep going with the ones who believed Facebook would not be the billion-dollar company that it is today. Facebook keeps loved ones connected over the entire world. Mark Zuckerberg kept enduring his fight no matter the circumstances of the way he planned for his vision to come to light. As long as you have faith in God and keep going, keep enduring no matter what detour unexpected twist your dreams will become your reality. We have all done it wrong before, as things come about. Unexpected twists arise in our plans and we created doubt by saying, *'It is not going to happen'*, or *'I'm just going to give up, it must not be for me '*. That doubt creates defeat allowing your unexpected twist become the focal point of now you make your next move typically not allowing you to move forward enduring one accepting the adversity that will bring forth the best outcome for your reality. When you focus on the problem instead of the ultimate goal the problem will expand because of what you focus on expands. One day I had planned to do a meeting in Statesville, NC for a fellow business partner to help promote and grow her business. Earlier that day I went to the ER and doubted they would be able to assist me as much as I need and honestly did not want to be waiting. I believe scheduling with my primary care doctor would be more beneficial with respect to time and accuracy. So, while waiting in the ER, I was able to schedule a doctor visit for the same day. It happened to be two hours from the current time. The time arrived for me to walk into doctor's office. I explained that I could only see out the corner of my eye everything else was pitched black and it started small and grew to me not being able to see out of my peripheral vision. When I finished explaining my doctor, in a nick of time, was able to schedule me an eye doctor appointment before the eye doctor close for the next day. I was excited about how she got me out. Fast enough to me to make it to Statesville. An hour and thirty minutes from Charlotte, I received a call from my doctor. She advised me to go to the ER. She believed my retina could possibly be detached and if so I could become blind if I went too much longer without having my eye looked at. I immediately went back and forth as I stressed over fact that I had an important meeting to attend. Should I go after she had urgently advised me to go to the ER? How I got off the phone with her and contemplated on how I could not let my new partner down. I made the decision ten minutes later that I would have faith and show up as I said I would. Although I was very nervous about my eye, I got to Statesville and accomplished the goal for the day. It was very difficult driving at night; being that I could only see out one eye. My right eye was hurting very badly. But it was worth pushing through and finishing what I started.

When I arrived at the ER at Carolinas Medical Center- University that night it was around ten. I was sitting in the lobby and remembered being there ten hours before. I had doubted if it was worth my time; and to be told to come back. You can only imagine how I felt on the inside.

I was overwhelmed. I felt like the day was wasted. After three hours of waiting the, doctor came in and explained the pictures of my eye. He told me that it didn't look good, that my retina was detached and that I had a giant tear in my eye. He also told me that I would need immediate surgery, and that there was no on- call surgeon present at that moment to perform the operation. I explained that my primary care physician had made an appointment for me the following day. I received the news that I could possibly lose my eyesight forever; that the surgery would be difficult, in my case. Time was not on my side. While shedding tears, I spoke life into my situation. I told myself that if this was the plan that God had for my eye then it would come to pass. If not, I would fight the battles that came with the process. I did not expect to hear that type of news that night. I could have given up and made excuses, or continued to inflict self-doubt. I could have told myself that my situation was going to lead to eventual blindness.

After I came out of surgery; this being my first surgical experience, I was glad to wake up. So many thoughts of fear of not waking up could have stopped me from gaining my sight back; not going into surgery because of doubt, worry and fear. My fate would be blindness. But I kept moving in faith, declaring that the best will come from this experience. I declared that I would endure as long as I had to, in order to get the results that wanted. Never give up, always keep going. If I would have let fear or doubt discourage me, I honestly know my experience would have been completely different. I trusted God and I know he gave me complete access to experience abundant life.

My doctor told me that the surgery was very rare for someone of my age and ethnicity. From the moment I found out that my retina was detached, until the moment after surgery my spirit and thoughts remained focused on only the best outcome. I shut every voice and thought that could have set a different outcome down. I only held onto the victorious one. I declared before I woke up that I would see out of my right eye again. I thank God that his plan for me was bigger than my current circumstances. As you read you see through some discouragement, but I pressed on in faith spoke words of life not sickness and grabbed hold of my belief. I have the faith that I will overcome all my fears.

This was a tough battle for me. I only had two people that I was really close to... but I had God. The surgery was just the beginning. After surgery, my eye doctor told me I had to be on bed rest for a week, until my next visit. Dr. Whiteman at Horizon Eye Care instructed me to always lay on my right side, emphasizing ***always***. To only get up four times per day; to go to the bathroom, eat, and shower and to take eye drops. I had to do everything lying on my right side. I absolutely never imagined me going through anything of such nature and the only thing going through my head was my business; how close I was to my next promotion… not been able to be present for my team and myself. Allowing me to heal and relax was the hardest thing for me to want to do. So many emotions of hurt and disappointment; I wanted to reconcile but the way my thought process and faith is I could not allow myself to grow. I was holding on to negative thoughts of what I was experiencing. But I did remind myself of how to remain humble and thankful, no matter how my plans changed or detoured. I kept pushing and was very intimate with the process. I did not want to tell my mother until after because I didn't want to give her additional stress. She had her own issues. She was very impulsive, so irrational at times due to her anxiety. I did not want the pressure as days carried on I did exactly as the doctor instructed. When the week was up, I started to begin to do normal activities again. I slowly began to drive. My eye was feeling better, even though I still had blurred vision because of the certain oil filters to keep my retina from detaching. I continued to stay positive, excited about what I knew was coming. I had planned this outcome before my surgery.

On my second week of recovery, no longer on bed rest, I turned my focus to my son. I was picking him up from practice when I received a phone call from a detective, asking me had I talked to my mother. I told him no. I had texted her two days prior, but she never responded. They went into detail on how they found her car in a public parking lot almost two weeks before. I immediately drove to her house to check on her. No one came to the door. There was a late rent notice. I raised my eyebrows, confused. I called my brother and family, expressing my concern. My brother had a key to her house, so he rushed over to her house for more answers. When he got there, he called me on Facetime. We looked through it together; stuff was kind out of place and the food in fridge was molded. He grabbed one of her cell phones that he had found and left. I explained to him that the way everything looked in the house was as if she had rushed out.

Later that night I called the detective back to gain more clarity since she wasn't answering anyone's calls. He also had me feeling some kind of way about the manner in which he had questioned me regarding my mother. His discrete manner made me feel like I was a suspect of some sort. I watch a lot of CSI, NCIS and Law & Order and I felt like I could identify the approach from detective a little clearer. I needed more clarity. The subtlety of the detective's questions along with my mother's apparent disappearance was not adding up for me. I began to ask questions...**What happened to my mama? Is my mom dead?**

The detective from the Mint Hill Police Department informed me that someone had called in about finding a body in the woods earlier that day.

"They did a finger print scan and your mother's name came up. She has some special distinctions. But before jumping to conclusion we want to make sure that it was her.", He tried to reassure me. When I confirmed some piercings and body construction, it was true. My mother was no longer alive. She had been in the woods for almost two weeks. Her body was not viewable and just perishing. At that moment there was so much confusion, so many questions, but most of all disbelief in the way plans I had for us would no longer be possible. The entire time of the last couple days of my bed rest my mom body was in the woods, all alone. During that moment I was numb but thankful for whatever the plans God had in store for my life.

My dad got shot and killed in 2014, when I was 6 months pregnant with my son Michael. Now five years later my mom was no longer here... unsolved and unknown. My thoughts could have caused me to shut down to give up on everything, but it put fuel to the fire. I have to keep pushing my child, my younger brother, my family... me and anyone else that has lost a parent. We all need to know how to keep looking forward and up. You can keep going, no matter the unexpected, no matter what life throws your way. When you think trials are here to stop you, put your head down and stay focus on the goal. Believe the best is yet to come. Believe that you can achieve your goals no matter the adversity. Believe in yourself and trust the process. Strive, push and please always keep going until you fulfil your destiny. The hand-picked life you want for you. It's going to always be roadblocks and humps in your road. It is destined for that, but God gave us complete access through His word; even through discouragement, trust and have faith.

Speak life into every area so you can have joy as adversity and twists come along. I will continue to press on and keep going until God calls me home; I do believe my destiny will come to pass. The lessons and strength come from the unexpected. Just breathe and live for the moments to come.

CHAPTER 3
BREATHE

T HIS YEAR, AS LIFE SHIFTED, DAYS went by; minutes went away, seconds
flew and all of the experiences had taken me in a thousand different
directions no matter the plans. I had learned to take a moment and just
breathe. During our experiences the only way to keep pushing with total
control is by taking a deep breath and enjoying the moment for what it
is. In the natural, we humans don't always understand that we *choose* to
react to what happens to us. In that moment, no matter what, I will always
choose to breathe. Do you recall getting worked up about things you have
no control over because you planned a different outcome? Sometimes we
tend to put more on ourselves than you have to endure when we don't
trust that God gave us complete access. March 2019 when my mother
Tanishua Lavonnda Sanders passed away during the time I planned to
hit a promotional rank in my company. I kept pushing, knowing that...
greater is he that is in me.

Live for every moment. God woke you up and gave you a break today.
He gave you breath to breathe and the fullness of life. When you can
get up, keep going; taking each moment for not even a second. I am so
grateful just for the moments that my family is able to wake up and speak.
I am grate for my family's ability to exist today with great health. Never
get carried away with anything other than living for a moment. You can
easily start living your life and forgetting to enjoy and embrace both the
good and bad. It is activities that can powerfully assist you in enjoying the
moment, like the ones you love to do. As you are pressing forward, doing
those activities that you love, that align with the hand-picked life that you
have to create continue to savor the memories that go along with it. Life

has its way of continuing you just breathe and let go of all the things that can have your focus distracted. Your experience during the process will become more exciting and joyful. Then it grows and starts to become more of what you make it.

Have a positive attitude as you live by taking moments and not forsaking your opportunities. Accepting the outcome that comes with the journey while you are wanting to go towards the reality you want to live. I absolutely can ensure that having negative, doubtful emotions. And conduct towards the unexpected twist will not change what is happening, ask yourself your negative behaviors when a something unexpected out your control came about now did it change the way the outcome happened? Realize the unfortunate happened look at it for the moment it is. Find and focus on the best in the situation that is in occurrence. Then make joy for the whole outcome as for what it is. Going through what you are going through regardless. Take a moment to breathe and find the happy place. Since the only thing you have full of control over is yourself. You will have your opportunity to always choose the choices of your character and being steadfast on trusting believing God is all you need. When you find yourself in a place on your way to work and you promised yourself you are going to wake up early be on time to work. As everything is going according to your plan while you are driving on the way to work then you hear horrible rubber sounds, looking in the mirror, your tire is flat. Now upset because you planned on being early. At that moment when you pull over is the most valuable. It creates your power in the full control over how the rest will affect you mentally, physically, and emotionally. At that moment you noticed in the side mirror that your tires are flat is the first opportunity where the choice comes for you to choose with make a decision on how you will allow your attitude to affect the circumstances. Coming from places of knowing how to handle emotions is not a consuming commonly know how to. It takes a ample amount of effort. When I first noticed the flat tire, before pulling over, I was no longer seeking frustration or anger. The **growth** is choosing to take a deep breath being thankful that you're a live, be thankful that it was not a collision, and that you have full access to everything that God has. It is best not to get caught in the problem that we see just continued to find the solution to what the plan or goal you have set. You can't go back to the time you left the house and start the drive to work over. You can't go back to avoid the thing that caused your tire to become flat no need to stay focused on the circumstances occurred. Tell yourself what it will bring me to have conflict towards the past. Would you now be able to just make circumstances disappear? The answer is no. You must embrace it; determine to get the need done for the outcome you have desired. Certain emotions contribute be inclination to great health. If can affect more than the current moment when not choosing the best perspective to live by. How you live has major effect on your long Gevity overall health. You can take for granted the moment it can hurt you for a lifetime in any aspects of your life. As children growing up our parents or an adult would tell us it going to be okay. When things could not turn in our favor for the things, we desired at the moment we desired it. As you become older life then and today it could be difficult to accept the fact that everything is and will be okay because of what you can physically see. It still goes along away today to know everything will be okay. If that becomes hard for you to accept in the natural you can accept always through Jesus, our Christ. You might not feel okay you might not see as it is okay, but it has to be okay. It is okay to just relax. it is okay to breath; it is okay to be thankful. It is okay that you will still be victorious. It is okay that you cannot change the unfortunate events that take part in your journey. Never waste energy on the things you have no control to be able to change. These occurrences are put in place to test your strength and faith. When you get ready to run a race you lace your strings and you go for it. No matter during the race if your strings untie you keep going even if you have to kick your shoes off to get to the finish line you are not stopping for no obstacle that came up. You keep going towards the finish line adjusting and aligning yourself doing whatever it takes until you make it. GO! GO! GO! Taking deep breaths, you stride with every ounce of everything in you. The voices said "tie your shoe" "you're going to fall "you kept going, believing in you not falling. Each moment I am going make it. "I can do it "as you kept going knowing God has you, coming in second place the encouragement the belief in yourself and trusting God you finish you made it through. Rejoice because your strength, you might not receive first place the way you planned or how you would normally because your adversities but guess what you got it is okay. You have shown your dedication and commitment to yourself. You have to see how not to experience that again. Most of all you kept your spirits high and maintained peace in all you do.

When giving your best, with regards to your circumstances; you can always be thankful and appreciate the way you carry it out. Understand that whatever tends to look like adversity in the natural, God is using it to show his presence in the spiritual. The prayer that allows me and guides me to be content during the journey is the <u>Serenity Prayer,</u> written by the American theologian, Reinhold Niebuhr, in 1951.

> ***"God grant me the serenity to accept the things I
> cannot change courage to change the things I can
> and have wisdom to know the difference."***

This particular prayer represents the calmness you can enjoy and peacefulness that will remain in you; when you go through life, living moment to moment for God. If you are a firm believer, God will always have his arms wrapped around you.

Let's say you caught a flat tire? Now most of us are going to be at least a little upset. Now, what if you knew that awaiting just ahead was waiting a T-bone collision that God didn't want you to be a part of. Would you still have negative thoughts toward the circumstances, or would you be grateful that you still had a vehicle... not in the hospital or in a collision that would hinder your next day's activities. If we could see what God knew, we would always be in a mode of humbleness and gratitude. When you are able to breeze your way through obstacles with trusting the process, letting go of everything; giving God full control by praising being thankful, all the weight of burdens is lifted. You are giving yourself the opportunity to experience abundance and to be free of worry, hurt, shame and guilt.

God does everything for a reason. He wants us to trust him. At that moment when you have to choose how we deal with the effect of the circumstances. This is the opportunity to initiate growth. This is the opportunity to trust him completely. Remember that it is all working for your good. Not one thing that comes up in your life to detour your peace will ever be for the greatest. God wants you to enjoy your best life, full of freedom. The perspective, or the glasses you look through, will either move you forward or keep you in the past. Each moment has passed away, for the next millisecond is a new moment. Never lose sight for staying on what was for what is to come is a blink of an eye away. It is a beautiful thing to understand we have more control over who we are than what happens to us. It is magnificent and extraordinary that we serve a great God; one that controls all of what happens to us. Life happens and shows up for everyone as soon as they take their first breath of air. God created the beginning and the end. We can run but what is to come now and then has our name on it. As long as we stand on God's rock, hanging on to his truths, we will have a great life. Everyone's life is different. Everyone is not supposed to be the same. God created your life especially for you. The handpicked reality that you choose to create you must believe God has for you. It will come to light. We have all phases in life where things change but that is already in God's plan. When you trust God you are able to be fulfilled and walk in a new light. You know that ***trouble endures for a night, but joy comes in the morning…*** through Christ. Nothing or no one can steal your moments of joy. ***Thy rod and thy staff comfort me,*** says the word of God. He gives us His word. His word is the truth. You can always locate His truths in the Bible. When you just relax and do the things you love to enjoy while on the road to victory you are giving yourself room to enjoy the experience. In those moments, on our way to our destiny; the miracles happen that forever change our lives, when we at least expected it be the most important piece to our life story. When we go through the adversities Gods placed in our lives, do not miss in the moments. These are the moments where the miracles happen. This is where God is setting you up for your next blessing. Opportunities are on the way. God places every person, place and thing in your life at the right time. Letting go of your thoughts of destruction towards everything comes with trusting and believing everything will work out. Once you choose the mindset of life over death, you will see the light in all aspects. Take a moment and close the book. Take every burden, any worries, and no matter how small or big and put it in the box. Close it, throw it far and exhale. Take two more deep breaths and tell God thank you for life.

Today, someone isn't going to wake up. Your situation is not at all bad if you're here to still change or improve it. We are winners, conquers of all things; because you have access to a wonderful God that is bigger than our problems. He created us to be at peace; no matter what the circumstances are. God has so much in store for you but he watches how you deal with your unfortunate twists that arise in your life. Are you breathing, having faith? Are you being wrathful and not being of good character? Your life becomes what you make it by the mindset you choose. You will not enjoy the fullness of your moments if you view the situation in a negative way, something else is blocking that causing you to miss the miracle. The goal is to conquer the miracles you do not know. God has the date... no one else does. With that being a certainty, stay focus enjoy the moments now. There is no promise for the next moment, as life happens. God has full control over all circumstances. And you have full control over yourself.

In the next moments of your life be assertive, be purposeful... be determined to always choose righteousness within self. Enjoy your life as it is and what is to come. You can say I love you after an argument before dinner and eat or you can walk out with anger coming back to ambulance your love one died choking on a piece of meat. Find out what is important to you and the handpicked reality you choose to create. Stay focused on moving forward in that direction, striding through adversities. Take the moment's adversities and learn from them. Take each moment as a gift, for the next moment is never promised. God loves us forever. We are his children. He gives us everything we need. We will be okay as long as we keep pressing on. Embrace the trees, the air you breathe and the love that surrounds you.

CHAPTER 4
LIVE. LOVE. LAUGH

YOU HAVE ACCESS TO ALL THINGS no matter what. God gave you everything he has through Jesus Christ. God wants you to experience the life that he promised us; the life of joy and favor and abundance. Abundance does not always equate to a specific amount. God has the blessings he wants you to experience. It is all the beautiful favor over your life that he grants to us by the simplicity of life. What does the phrase, **to live,** actually mean to you? What does it look like to you **to live**? What does it feel like to you **to live**? As you are here on earth I ask you these questions to see what perspective you choose without recognizing if that is the perspective you want. We all have our own way we choose to live our life but do we understand what it means to actually live. You could be here on earth waking up day by day handling responsibilities but ask yourself does that really mean that you are living your life? You can be moving but not fully living. You can be waking up but not fully living. You can be breathing and not be living. Living fully is being grateful for all aspects of life… living through Christ, as long as you are living happily no matter the circumstances. Doing what makes you happy, smiling because you can. Crying because you can but knowing that God has all your tears and each one that sheds he has something in store for it. Living fully is waking up with intent being intentional with your day moving on purpose you have 24 hours considered to be in a day. Are you thankful when you wake up for being able to wake up that morning? What ways are you showing yourself that you are appreciative of the next 24 hours. What ways are you giving God his praise for him awakening you this morning?

God's gift to us is life. What we do with it is our gift to him. When we are complaining, not satisfied, we are not living to our fullest potential. We are taking moments away from experiencing a great moment. Living your life to the fullest, with the access that you have through Christ means you're creating the best experience through grace, mercy and joy… however the situation looks. Living is continuously being joyous in astronomical places. Taking the highroad over when you can take the road to keep misery. Christ lives through you as long as you believe. He never no matter the circumstances did not move in any spirits other than Grace. During the times that it takes the greatest trick than what you had to remain humble and enjoy it you can always remember you have God's strength. You deserve the joy to live because Christ is within you. He says, **'greater is he that is in me."**

Smiling helps others around you to smile and live a joyous life. This in turn creates experiences that more than just about you. This causes fulfillment in your life. How many times a week are you complementing or helping the ones around you? How many times in a day are you complementing of bringing joy to yourself? How many times are you smiling just for small things you overlook because you are constantly moving? How many times are you frowning during your week? How many times in a day are you complaining about the past? How many daily affirmations are you speaking to your life each day? How many thoughts of victory do you create when adversities come about? Every day you asked yourself these questions to ensure you stay in alignment to live fully.

The more you participate in your life, to live your best life, the higher the number of affirmations, compliments and serving others through joyous spirit. The lower the numbers decline to zero, where it is no longer a number for you frowning, complaining, and focused on your past you will see firsthand experiencing a gracious life. The settlement of life is the axcess we have through Jesus Christ who has control. Knowing who you are will lead you to being above ground level. God is who you are and Jesus Christ his son is in you who believe. God has full control over all things. God gives us access to all things. He has access because he loves us. He wants us to be powerful. We have everything already that we need to be powerful, joyful, and graceful. Having access through Christ means that if the doctor tells you that you have an incurable disease but you declared knowing God's power. It means that you will be healthy, because you know that God says his children are healed through the blood of Jesus. Axcess creates the power inside of you to know that you are mighty because you come from a Mighty One who created you and all your ancestors. When any form of rejection comes knowing because you have access that it does not confirm to you because you chose to believe in God for his word is true. Trust the process to gain access. Now you have everything you need and more through Jesus' blood to handle what comes your way. To work in your favor when the bills are due and unexpected unknown Checks come in the mail you know when that things happen on the right time because God gave you full access. When you have no food in your fridge but a friend called and invited you over for dinner. Thank God because he gave you full access to abundance. You are spared from going hungry, when it is someone else that will go hungry at the same time your friend called.

Knowing that because God gave you access you may not have the transportation you want to make it to work but you have health to be able to endure public transportation. With minimal effort, God is the way I live my life. The power I witnessed in my life through the access God granted me allowed doors to open for me that would never open on my own or would have taken much longer. God's access in my life had workers tell me that it's nothing else can be done and then trusting in God working towards the goal then everything that someone stated it is not possible, but God had a different outcome for my situation. God says yes to us it Might not be at the Times we need it but it's on his time according to his plan. You have to continue to believe in his greatness knowing that you have access to everything you need now and to come. When we as humans lack patient that is a liability takes away from experience a life of full access and living fully. If you are asking, how does patience create a barrier in experiencing a full life that you have access to through Christ? Think about the times when you were rushing wanting things to hurry and go your way fast as you wanted. Think about a time when things you were not being patient about. Did you rush your way to a different outcome? Out of the outcome did the experience leading up to the outcome cause you peace? Did it cause you to have others joyous? Did you just trust God? As I am being an authentic witness to what the access, we have through Christ has done for me. It brings me great satisfaction to say he can do it for you too. We are worthy and more than enough for God regardless of how we feel.

God desires for us to live through him, being filled with his grace and mercy. God loves you unconditionally no matter how your circumstances seem to be he loves who he created you to be. God loves who you are and what you are even when you do not love it yourself. God wants us to love ourselves the way he loves us. Love is a four-letter word that has control and power to our life and contributes to the way we receive God's access. Love is within us to receive and reciprocate. What does love mean to you? Who are you choosing to live? What are you choosing to love? How are you being involved in love throughout each day? What type of love do you want to experience? How often are you telling yourself how you love yourself? How are you showing others love? Love makes the world go around. Love creates life. Love shows passion. Love is action. Action means to act. Love is shown through various ways which creates special moments and experiences. Jesus Christ shows us the ultimate example of the love he had for his father children by coming on earth as a man to show us what it looks like to be a child of God. The circumstance Jesus was put into was for the love of his father; and to teach others the way of life, living through the Holy Spirit. God loved us so much that he gave his son to be crucified on the cross for forgiveness of our sins. God love for us has forgiveness, he wants us to follow his commandments but he knows we are not perfect. When we do something that does not align with his commandments or the obeying his word that is considered to be sin. God Still has unconditional love for us and wants us to know we can love him unconditionally by just obeying his word.

God's love for us has patience. He waits on us to be obedient to his word because he knows he gave us free will to believe in him as our Lord and Savior. When times come up that you doubt God's word is true and focus on doing things your way in the natural space God still has patience for you by providing grace upon you that he will be careful still in how he cares for you until you obey him and his commandments. God's love for us has kindness. He wants us to be selfless in kindness and how we treat others... ***and ourselves.*** In those times when we hurt ourselves knowing that contributes to not living through Christ. God shows us his selflessness through his actions towards us by providing for us regardless of how we handle someone as long as we ask for forgiveness. When Jesus was born his walk on earth shows us how being selfless to those who choose him giving us the way to see how to remain humble and selfless to every situation brought forth to us. God love is the way to live. The humane world we live in has the capability to manipulate what the true version of love is. I assure you that if you complete access God love is the only way to love. People come from different backgrounds, life experiences, and places which have a major role on how they choose to love. Never take it personal did God did not create or give us the same life experience to everyone. It will always be a different detail in your story then the next persons. Minor or major detail but it is different which causes us to be different from each other. God loves and choosing his way allows all that choose him to now have the same qualities of the one and only his son Jesus Christ. God love for you shows you how to love yourself and others. Love is not the way your parents taught you, not the experiences you have, not the way you determine. God love is patient, kind, honest and unconditional. That is the type of love you have to produce that grants you the opportunity to have complete access. You can easily find yourself not loving yourself the way God loves you. God gives us access to be great. By you having access to be great and you choose things that is not exemplify that, would you say you are loving yourself fully or unconditionally? Have you ever took opportunities for granted? Have you ever made goal for improvement and not give it your all to reach your goal? Have you ever told someone you would help and then telling them you cannot because you just do not feel up to it anymore? Have you ever tell yourself that you are unworthy or disgusted with attributes of God created you with? Have you ever disrespected someone because you were hurt by them? Have you ever live for your satisfaction of what you need or want? Have you ever put others in a harmful position for your own selfishness controlling position? Have you ever held on in your heart to what pain others caused you? Have you ever not got up out the bed because of you being upset about unfairness you focused on? Have you ever not gave your all in what you are doing? Have you ever not eaten because you were upset about the past (anything that is behind the moment you are currently in)? Have you ever ignored a love one because they did not agree with you or you did not agree with them? Have you ever not wanted to wake up or felt not living any longer due to your circumstances? If the answer is yes to any of these questions you are not participating in God's love and how he wants you to love yourself and others fully. Love means a lot to us as humans whether we need now or never want to feel that way it does matter. Loving yourself is very important but can be very difficult to do, because it isn't what you know how to do. When you love yourself because God loves you, the perspective of how you are to love yourself aligns with God's love.

What does it mean to truly love you, the way God does? It means to show you your best self. Know that God wants you to experience the most of life living through him. It should never be a reason, even if in the natural, that you could have a legitimate disdain for life. You should always want to wake up because you have complete access. When you choose to be down you are not being grateful for God's love for you. Is the only reassurance and validation you need to be wonderfully amazingly you. Nothing should be able to ever take you from a space that will have you not been one with God love is to you. You want to first hold on to God's love and then spread it. Show yourself and no matter how I'm living towards my handpicked reality I will continue to live in God's love. Be honest with yourself and others. Love yourself by striving for greatness, attacking in each goal with passion and humbleness with regards to the stumbling blocks in the journey, eating healthy, moving with purpose because God gave your breath to do everything that aligns with greatness. Love others how you want to be love. God says to love thy neighbor. When it comes to the way God wants us to love, he does not want you to only love yourself. He cares about the way you love others because it shows your character towards his people and character of your heart. The more you are selfless, the more access you will have through Christ. It becomes difficult in the natural to be selfless because we as humans think of what is being taken or use from us but we trust and believe that God is all we need he will show favor and multitudes for us of being in his word to be selfless. Love is more than how we feel, it is how we act. If God loved us only when he felt like it we would be in trouble. Love to God has nothing to do with how it makes our heart feel only the way we act towards his creations… when we are caring towards others with compassion. When I give I never want my focus to be what will I get in return you immediately declined the value of what you are what you will receive. I always remind myself what God has for me is better than what I or someone has for me. If it is meant for you to receive it will never be forceful. God just gives without hassle for the reward and access comes from the endurance being obedient. Spread God's love without no expectation of return from others. You are what matters most on the day God will judge you. Continue to act in his ways regardless of others. The love that you have will allow you to become one with God having complete access to his life of abundance in it. Love yourself not your circumstances. You get lost in the world and where you are destined to be if your current circumstances have control over how you act. It is only way to carry out the way to love which we know is God's love. It will not matter if you had reach your goals, if you are far from what you want in life, if you are hurt, if you are healed, if you are healthy, if you have diseases, If you are rich and if you are broke. You are still required to love yourself and others the way God tells us to. This is very clear in his word, in order to have total access. Love when others choose hate, love when others shows selfishness, love when everything falls apart, love when your plans had unexpected changes, love when something or someone afflicts pain, love when life gives you reason to give up, love and you have no money, love when you are sick, Love when we have no transportation, love when your loved ones pass, love when you are alone, love when you get fired, love when you get robbed, love when you've been raped, love when you've been heartbroken, love through every adversity and love through every reward. Once you become great at giving Gods love when the way life unexpected twist, doubt fear, every day moments will become more for fulfilled and with purpose. You can enjoy the moments; you can live for each aspect of moments because Love gives us fulfillment. As we live our life to God's love we have the blessings to choose how we want our emotions to be doing every moment. What we practice becomes habit and habit becomes character. As we continue to love ourselves and others, another principle that gives a fulfilling life is laughter. Laughing is a fundamental creates show signs of joy. Recall a time you are out with a group of friends from having a long day at work and you enjoying each other's company enduring laughter with great times as time goes by do you forget all of the rest of the day or do you focus on your day? Have you ever called your friends and family to make you laugh or Bring you joy because you wanted to have a joyous experience? Laughter brings us to a place that will continue to have us in a great spirit. Laughter decreases stress hormones and increasing immune cells and infection fighting antibodies. Laughter boosts the immune system. A good hearty laugh relieves physical tension and stress leaving your muscles relaxed for up to 45 minutes after. It increases energy levels, improves memory and alertness. Laughter, like smiling is the shortest distance between you and another person. It makes us feel closer to each other it creates a bond. Laughing is great at all times when adversity comes up it is a form of outlet. When in it unexpected twist arises are you choosing laughter or anger? Do you believe in laughter or happiness during your life? What ways are you creating an experience for you and others to feel the joy of happiness being fulfilled? As we know laughter has different roles in our body mentally, physically and emotionally. We can feel nervous, anxious and still create laughter. I am a silly person most would say. All my family says that I'm always laughing. I do agree and for me over the years it has showed me that it is my outlet natural without it being a practice for my lifestyle. Ironically it has it awkward moments because it looks as if in the natural viewing the circumstances as a joke or playful when it's not the reason. In today's society most of humans has no control over the emotions to the circumstances. The circumstances control their emotions, who their character becomes, what's the next move made. But, discipline in controlling emotion to create your circumstances. Imagine you falling in a workplace and your Coffee goes flying in front of everyone in the break room what you choose to react next will determine how the circumstances affect you. If we take the time to breathe and understand everyone makes mistakes or have accidents we have no room to be ashamed or feel defeated. If we laughed at our own situation as we are enduring the impact of everyone else feelings loses power on how it can make you feel. No shame as others take the circumstances, however you can laugh and rejoice even in pain because you have access to Jesus Christ. He wants to make the best out of what the world will consider to be the worst. Laughing your way humbly through your journey on your way to the handpick reality you create gives you a peaceful experience. Everything good or bad that comes my way has been defeated through my choice of laughter. I honestly do not know what has led me to find laughter in all outcomes since I was little girl but as an adult I enjoy it more especially finding it to be a rare thing many adults does not currently know how to conquer. In professional settings I have to practice becoming more subtle due to my results always having a laugh. It is a working progress but I'm perfect through Christ to God. So it means nothing as long as I am not causing harm and I am obeying God I will accept my great spirit regardless of any circumstances. As long as you operate your plan in the spirit of Christ, all doors will remain open for you that aligns with your destiny. Walk in your destiny with knowing to always laugh because God always has control over your circumstances by you just walking in his spirit. Life moments are precious. When you just learn to live and take care of yourself, loving everything about your life growing towards everything you have to do. In every aspect of your life God wants you to experience him he desires for you to experience him he desires you to live love and laugh through every trial, and all tribulations. Never forget your first priority after giving God his glory is to LIVE without no regrets or even contemplating with your past. When you are not trusting God, you are now saying that you are not thankful for your now and what's to come. Yes just talking, thinking or wishing about regrets things that could have, should have, or would have had already have so just trust God that it's everything that's has have is according to his plan that will bring peace unto your life. Peace to know that it is everything in the now. Now life; not tomorrow, not when you get your next check, not when you feel like it, live NOW for that moment is yours. You owe it yourself to do those things that make you happy and to embrace the way you live through Christ. When you decide to be free, to enjoy life for what is dealt smiling, helping others, and not subsiding you're vision for no one but GOD.

When you choose to live your best life through Christ the journey becomes easier. The road to loving thyself and thy neighbor is refreshing to do because you know how God loves and provides for you. The process to being filled with laughter becomes a character and not just a time when you are watching tv. You are creating memories of great, times with your loved ones sharing laughter. The way of life is a lifestyle of character that is purposefully intentionally created. That gives you full access through Christ for what God will do for you. Move intentionally towards love. God loves teach us how we can love our way through our journey.

Giving to others no matter our circumstances and letting go of all things that does not promote the life you want, the love you give and the way you want to live through Christ. Your life will not and was not intended to be the same as anyone you know. Enjoy the beautiful life you have. When you truly love anything you normally embrace it. When we embrace every aspect of our now life we are telling God we deserve the abundance of all we ask for and what he has already gave us. Live now, love forever, and laugh often.

CHAPTER 5
THE JOURNEY

I'M GOING THROUGH THE JOURNEY OF life with these three principles: Live, Love and Laugh. These principles enable me to experience the access that God grants us our journey. This will always remain purposeful. We all have our own journey through life. Every day the choices we make creative journey we experience. Each moment created is an experience. Experiences are things that create the journal you are leaving. Everything happens for a reason and serves a purpose in our life. You go to life learning lessons, from mistakes, gaining endurance, wisdom, and insight. The journey of life is what you make it. In every aspect of your life you have the opportunity to choose how you react. Through your journey of experiences when life gives you lemons make lemonade. This is so true and a great way to understand what you go through can be sour and not of great flavor but we have the ability to sweeten it up, making the best of it with different tools which creates the great taste we know as lemonade. To have fulfillment and join the axis you have through Christ that he gives us because we believe it's in looking at the lemonade in all circumstances that you are in. Breathe and trust God during your journey. A week and some days before I got the news my mother passed away during the time on bed rest someone close to me did not follow through on a payment agreement. Never did I imagine going through the pain as my only intention was to help her out to be able to get a car & in that moment I felt as if it backfired on me.

During that time in March 2019 while being on bed rest until March 8 my bills are becoming delinquent because at the time I was a full-time self employed. Which means make money for myself... by myself so it was not physically participating in what creates the income I will not obtain any financial gain. Prior to me being on bed rest February 28th my son caught the flu in the middle of February three days before the big event CIAA was being hosted in my city. On a regular week it would have not caused much of an issue. Two months prior I leased my apartment on Air BNB for the two biggest events In North America basketball event which is CIAA and All Star.

I was so excited that that guest booked my place and I made my first sale for both events. My intentions were to stay with a friend as my guest stayed in my apartment alone. My mind was now racing, full of possible solutions, due to my son Michael having the flu. I didn't want to cancel the reservations. That would not be fair. So I calculated the income in planning for my upcoming bills. I prayed and hoped for Michael O'Neal to get better before we had to evacuate the apartment. As the days went on, Michael was not well enough for me to move him out of my place... even temporarily. *'I'll call my mom'*... she didn't pick up. I called my friends and pleaded. Of course, no one wants to catch the flu so they hesitated which is understandable. A lot of thoughts were still running through my mind. Michael and I were able to stay with a friend. Thank God.

My apartment was basically rented out for six days, two different bookings. I began to thank God for seeing us through, to be able to have somewhere else to go and still being to get the goals accomplished. I honestly did not want to be at this particular friend's house with my sick child for long because I knew conflict could have arisen. Trusting in God and having faith allowed me to continue to go through with my decision; being able to remove my pride and humble myself. Michael still sick as a couple days pass by and what I did not want to go through I went through. My friend shared words with me about Michael being sick and us being at their place. So uncomfortable, I left and now back to ground one. Again, I have nowhere to go, my mom is still not picking up the phone and no one wants my son in their presence. He has the flu. The option I favored the most that would give me full peace of not being a burden on anyone; because my responsibility as being a mother, a care provider remains the same no matter the circumstances was to booking a hotel. Now reviewing the dynamics in my mind it, is the most inflating week in Charlotte for rooms. All to most hotels are sold out or room where double to triple in pricing. Charlotte, North Carolina's weather was cold and all around extra costly that weekend. I thought to myself, at least if I pay I will be comfortable and warm.

I made the decision to drive at least six hours to Florida. I still didn't have a city right, but why not be in a place that made me happy. After making the decision that day, I began driving the next six hours to Florida. After checking the weather in different Floridian cities, Daytona became my first choice because it would be the hottest. During the time I made sure Michael was as comfortable as possible. I still giving him medicine and keeping him hydrated. As we approached Daytona I found a hotel online that appeared to be suitable for us and our circumstances. Finally we arrived. We pulled up to the hotel. I go to the counter to reserve a room and clerk told me that they were '*...sold out tonight*' and the rates are **doubled**.

I immediately asked the attendee why was the room sold out and she explained that this was the weekend for Daytona 500 NASCAR race. I said," ...Oh my, I was leaving my city because a big event. I went back to the car...s it's two in the morning, almost three. I reevaluated my thoughts and plans because my goal now is to never spend more then I came to save... **and be warm.** After reevaluating, I just relaxed. At this point, I'm starting to feel overwhelmed. And that would definitely not help me or my son Michael. I decided there will be no need to look for hotels any longer in Daytona and I was very tired. Michael was asleep, so we slept in the car in a parking spot at the hotel until the sun came up. I woke up to face the morning sun. It was so warm. I couldn't be more excited, taking in each moment. I thought to myself, *where to next*. I realized that it was Sunday. To me and my household, Sunday means church. No matter where I'm at, if it's possible, on Sunday I shall attend church and worship God.

Realizing that it was Sunday I immediately began to google churches. But I'm still particular when it comes to choosing anything I participate in. So at first I googled churches near me; then I googled New Bethel Ministries where I currently attend in North Carolina. One appeared but I did not know if it was under the jurisdiction of my bishop and C.O.G.I.C church. I was a little skeptical until a light bulb went off and I remembered another church I volunteered at and attended regularly, named Elevation Church. They had a location in Florida. Ecstatic, I found an Elevation Church in Melbourne, Florida. It was about an hour and a half away from Daytona. I cranked the car and began driving to church. Not caring about anything other than my son Michael and I being a part of a great worship on Sunday morning, fellowshipping in God's name. We pulled into the parking lot and were greeted in the way we were greeted as if we were at home in Charlotte. We experienced the love from the volunteers and staff. They told us where to go and what to do. Michael still wasn't feeling well. I had a phenomenal time, listening to the word of God placed into Pastor Steve's heart to deliver to us.

While I was in church, nothing but the grace and favor that God gave was on my mind. I was so thankful to have the transportation to be able to just jump up and go. I was thankful that my son was still here. I was thankful for him making away for us now then and in the present. I was thankful for safe travels he carried us through. I was thankful for healing, peace, and restoration. No problem that I could have experienced mattered at that moment. To me, as long as my son was breathing, life was great. When church let out and I was back in the car, never having been in Melbourne Florida before I GPS'd the nearest Wal-Mart to get Michael something to eat… medicine, snacks and juice to help Michael get better. After leaving Wal-Mart, still not having found a hotel for the day, I got Michael a bag situated in the car. I gave him a sandwich and some juice while I searched the app from my travel club that allows discounted hotel booking same day. I wanted to see which hotels and prices I could find in the area. I decided to stay in Melbourne due to the fact that Michael is sick and we did not need to be in the car any longer. I found a hotel not too far from Wal-Mart and I looked through the booking application. Once it was booked we drove about 10 miles until we arrived at the hotel. Pulling into the hotel the outside was not what I would have normally settled for, but during a season of spiritual growth, I remained humble. Arriving at the front desk, I gave my reservation number to the clerk. I was very surprised about his customer service and the way he handled his guest before me. It was soothing feeling and always a desirable transaction to have someone doing what they do well. He told me the price for my room and said he never seen that price before… that was a great rate. I got excited for the perks of being a Dream Trips member. Michael and I pulled to the door and entered the room. After getting him in the room I started removing the bags from the car, placing them in the room and parked the car. Walking to the room I had a breath of fresh air, inhaling and exhaling…

at peace. No one knows where I'm at it's just me and my son even though he was sick. I plan to start writing up and completing for the weekend it while Michael slept and enjoying the moment. I put our things up and live a nice candle from Wal-Mart. Finally able to wash peacefully I put Michael in the shower, cut the TV on for him to take a shower. Laying in the bed and grab my notebook and pen. 30 minutes later I got distracted, and this strange feeling in my hand came about in between my thumbs and point fingers. I no longer was writing a book I told myself I wake up and do it because of tired. I knew in my head that that was not the best idea if I was going to be serious about my goal. One thing I do know is God wants to works diligently and steadfast in your life always. When morning came the next day he was quickly getting back to normal. He saw Disney on the TV and said I want to go to Disney World. I jumped for joy, so happy that his dream was finally aligned with my bucket list for us. I told him we would go for his birthday that is in October. The year prior for his birthday I wanted to take them to Disney World but he insisted on Chuck E. Cheese. Not eager to compromise, I was willing to do it being his day of pleasures. In the moment, I was thankful that I did wait. There is no greater joy to me than to fulfill the desires of his heart when I am able to. I was waiting since birth or even before because I always wanted go to Disney but I did not so as a parent that was in my duty. It was time to leave Melbourne, packing things in car after getting dressed for check out time. The new location was Miami, Florida we went to the beach sat and while eating our snacks. Met some new friends and created some experiences with the ocean. We were just cruising the day away, living for the moment. It began to rain a little drizzle when we got in the car. So I drove to Orlando Florida for the next destination after researching things to do for Michael to play. I chose the Water Park in Orlando Florida and the weather was still great. Driving to Orlando Florida there were tolls that I did not go through before not prepared for fee only having minimal change and a debit card. It was a unexpected twist now people are beeping at me for I am lost if I have no change at the passing of the second toll. Employment tells me that she can't write a ticket and I will have to pay double and by mail. Driving away in disbelief as I approach another toll again not having cash and they do not take cards. Instead of losing my mind going crazy frustrating, just breathing I told the cashier I do not have change and yet they gave me another ticket. Happy we are still getting to go through the tolls, I embrace the warmth, windows down Michael sleeping in the car seat we arrive at the amusement park in Orlando Florida.

We went to the park Met the Jackson family mother Grandmother and her two grandkids. Michael played with them and sat with the children of the family. Having a great time enjoying myself as a big kid most would say. Being adventurous on rides I would never ever in my life think to ride. One that I had chances to experience called boomerang it takes you all the way to the top on a water raft and shoot you all the way down the rest of the way. It was nerve wrecking considering the rad tight with speed and I'm not a fan of rides at all. The encouragement from nine, 10, 11 year olds gave me all the adrenaline needed to for fill the task. Yes I can say I did it! I did it!! It's so funny to me because never in 1 million years would I'm not find excuses to why I will not get on the road. So many mechanical issues can go wrong, so many things can happen like me flying out of the ride it had no net but guess what I can say I pulled it off I did it! I conquered my own fear of rides and just living for the moment. It was the best decision as I rode with the granddaughter of the Jackson because it was two person rides only despite the situation of the past and the present I am having a blast. As it is approaching time for us to gather our belongings, now heading to the car. The weather was now changing; the sun was setting for the day. We dried off and changed from our wet clothes in the car. Pulling out the parking lot I see a Chuck E. Cheese, Michael insists to go play having more fun. As I told you before if I can get the job done of giving him his desires, it will get done. We park at Chuck E. Cheese we walked inside and Michael face lights up with a smile. Michael eyes are glowing and enormous. Ecstatic to play he gets ready for his play pass token letting the games begin. Once we finished playing games, Chuck E. comes out making all the kids run towards him. Chuck E. starts to throw tickets everywhere all the kids including Michael was going for them all. It was a pleasurable sight to see after him not feeling well. Michael and I left out of Chuck E. Cheese and went next door to a tourist shop. Michael and I traveled to Miami, Florida when he was just one year old. So this was his second time in Florida. The moments were very special to me that we were encountering together. We had to have souvenirs to take home with us. I absolutely love traveling and buying gifts. We walked around; Michael picking out toys, cups, shoes, and clothes that he liked. I grabbed me some gifts for myself and a few others items, taking my time to be thoughtful. Then we got to the register to check out and my stomach starts to ache from hunger pains. Michael was hungry too. We stopped again at two more shops to pick up a few more items for me.

As a child I can never recall us buying souvenirs when we traveled different places, but I always wanted to experience it, and those are the shopping trips that became the most significant to me. Once we finished shopping for souvenirs all we needed was to enjoy a good meal. Utilizing Dream Trips on my phone I discovered there were several places affiliated with the company that offered me the opportunity to discover new and exciting places. In addition, Dream Trips had about five choices of food places to choose from in the immediate area. I am choosing one of the five would be my greatest task as only accredited places are allowed to be affiliated. My biggest pet peeve is paying for food that is not quality tasting. The restaurant on the Dream Trips app that won the challenge after looking at menus was Sweet Frog. Sweet Frog was about 20 minutes away from our location. We pulled up to Sweet Frog.

We were met inside by a bouncer. So I second-guess if my son could go inside due to him being four years old. I walked up to the bouncer and asked if children could come inside, he said it was OK. I Grabbed Michael, we walked in and my mouth dropped. The inside is beautifully unique. At the door after walking in we were greeted by the host. We picked the seating of our choice. There were neon lights, artistic colorful paints on the wall, quotes on the ceiling that were on board every which way covering the whole ceiling, so creative nothing like I've ever seen before. Since it in the middle of the floor it's a big statue of a green frog with his heart out for a hug. Michael and I walk past the frog walking to the table of our choice noticing everyone with their balloon hat that was on top of their heads. We approached the table to sit down and here comes a nice guy walking up to us. He had balloon equipment in his hands and asked Michael what kind of balloon he wanted… he said Spiderman. I thought that would be impossible. But he got the balloons rolling, pulling them out of his caddy one by one. The last balloon made Spiderman's head actually which had a mask on it. It just blew my mind to not be at a fair or a kid's park to have that intriguing of a balloon made with it being a hat sitting on his head.

When he finished he sat a live balloon, full body Spiderman, on Michael's head... so amazed. He created me a flower. You could just know I was thrilled about my Dream Trips app and the decision I made to eat at this particular restaurant.

A waitress came to serve us. Going out to eat with me is a struggle within itself I'm absolutely indecisive so I did not know what to order to eat. Michael was still feeling a little not like himself but extra tired from such a fun-filled, long successful day. He knew that he wanted to order fries and chicken tenders. Putting his orders in first, we heard a loud voice over the speakers through the microphone saying the second raffle giveaway to five days in Cancun get your tickets out. I looked around as the patrons at the table beside me were fumbling gathering the tickets. The host starts calling numbers off the winning ticket. The woman at the table beside me starts screaming, overly happy that she won the raffle. I personally jumped for joy with her, gave her a hug and took a picture that was a blessing for her. God says to *rejoice for thy neighbor*. Within 10 minutes Michael was asleep on the table. Since it was very nice scenery I decided to take pictures. Grabbing my little blue sign out of my purse, I went towards the frog and asked the security guard to take the picture for me. I kept a close eye on Michael as he slept. I posed to take a picture holding my blue sign. As I was walking back to the tables, ladies asked about my blue sign that reads *"you should be here."* She told me that she was also was a part of my company and the conversation got deeper about the company. She knew some of the same leaders, working side-by-side with them, helping watch the Florida State we were in. Blessed to meet her, we laughed. I continued to watch Michael as he slept. I took a picture with her and she said a special greeting through a video we did to our friends that she had not seen or heard from in a long time.

The food has arrived. Michael began to eat when his food. While he was eating, my food had not arrived yet. I was just looking around noticing some more extravagant scenery I begin to take more pictures and ask the officer to take one of me with just ceiling quotes directly in front of the table we were sitting at. Noticing how I was smiling for the picture a lady who had arrived 10 minutes prior walks up to Michael from the table beside us. I asked her how I could help her as her table was the only one there besides three people at the bar.

She immediately started to attack me about my shower accusations as I said this was my child and I have him as she gets louder when she starts explaining her credentials of being a part of CPS (Child Protective Services). I was looking at her in shock and disbelief that she tried to state her case to me on how I'm choosing to direct my son. I had started to get worked up and I calmed myself down because my child was still in the presence of this calamity. The employees came over as her table began to attack me. I still want to see her credentials information to make a report. Her table was in overflow of alcohol glasses, the server was calming the table down as they were still screaming about my child being in the lounge. She refused to give me her credentials because she knows by law she cannot act out and make threats identifying work credentials, she continued to refuse to give me information.

Remaining levelheaded almost catching myself pointing and acting out of character, I left the situation alone no longer asking for information as her server attempted to diffuse the matter I ask for a to go box. Nice survey gave me the bill. I boxed my food, a bit came out during the nonsense after eating only one fajita. The food at Sweet Frog is absolutely delicious. I got my phone out and opened my lovely Dream Trips app to pay for our awesome food through the app, because the members of Dream Trips receive points towards their next vacation. I took Michael and my 'to go' boxes and left the Sweet Frog. Contemplating on whether we should stay another night or go home. I received a text message earlier that day from the guest in my house who had rented through Air Bnb, stating that they had to leave earlier then when the stay was already booked for.

Luckily God provides me with great people who surround me so he can show his favor. Made a phone call reaching out to my neighbor again; the first time being when the first guest left to help tidy up the place for the new guest and for the second time and to lock the door to my house once the last set of guest left. Very thankful and blessed for my neighbor he did not have to be there for me giving Tom the door key to my house; otherwise it would have remained unlocked. Just imagine coming back home to an empty house… all I can say is but God. Making the decision to stay another night or drive back to Charlotte, North Carolina was based on the value of how able I was to drive. Assessing the magnitude of the circumstances my tiredness was at the minimal which means we are heading back home to our beds. I made sure Michael was buckled in comfortably and he needed anything else before driving off. During the ride back home my right hand between my thumb and pointer finger had a little sharp pain. It was nothing visible, just a pain that came and left us as it pleased; me not knowing what was really going on with my hand but I kept pressing. Driving, pushing through the highways to arrive home. Now time was approaching that we needed gas. I didn't even recognize it, with less than 5 miles to the gas, I was on E as the dashboard mileage blinks. There was no gas notification sign in sight, and me with only 5 miles of gas left. Finally after a few miles an exit sign directing to the right with was service stations. I immediately turned in thanking God we did not break down ready to ride home. After pumping gas, throwing trash out, my now filthy road trip car sand everywhere, giving Michael some more medicine we drove back towards the highway for home.

It was 2AM. No more than an hour out I decide to call a friend because I was getting very sleepy and wiry. Talking with my friend was keeping me focused on staying awake. I finally arrived at the house at almost 3:45AM. It is wet cold and rainy in Charlotte. I got Michael out of the car leaving everything for the morning to remove. It is officially bedtime. Placing Michael in his room with the doors locked, no guest was available to go in his room. I slept with him that night. We woke up in the morning and Michael was feeling much better… more back to himself. Not leaving the house especially with Michael just feeling better, the temperature with the rain was not a great idea to me so we stayed in the house for the day. My hand was still bothering me.

Rubbing where the pain was like a weird, unexplainable, uncomfortable feeling. Time persisted as my hand was not feeling better it seems there's a little white flat bump inside my skin where it felt uncomfortable. I decided when I was in the shower to squeeze my hand massaging it thinking it would feel so good with the hot water running. Once night came my thumb and that area close to it between my pointing finger was bigger than it normally is. I laid down, massaging my hand and ignoring my friend's suggestion to go to the doctor. I waited until morning because of the weather conditions and the lateness of the hour. I didn't want Michael out in the night air. I dealt with the circumstances, just wanting this to be over. The pains were growing more and more severe. Michael and I wake up early to head out going to urgent care because it is faster than the emergency room. We walked in. I registered myself. The wait is about almost an hour. I learned that they opened one hour earlier than I thought. When the nurses and doctors came in to get me from the lobby they assessed me. The doctor told me I had cellulitis; an underlying skin infection from bacteria. It can come from being bit by a bug with other scenarios. Explaining to him how the problems I was experiencing started, he said he did have an idea what caused me to get it but they would be prescribing me antibiotics to take. It was time to go after he gave me my prescription. Across the street, there was a CVS pharmacy. We headed out. I go get the prescription then headed home and started to take the medicine when we got in the house. Michael at this point, all the way to himself, was laughing, playing, running, and doing what a four year old does. But I am in so much pain in my hand. Not being able to play with Michael or be that much attentive the way it throbbed. Devastated because it was my right hand, the hand I do everything with mainly my right hand which only makes sense because I am right handed.

The medicine prescribed was to be taken four times a day. Taking one when I picked up prescription at pharmacy to now time has went past it being almost 10 PM my hand only feeling worse, and it looks as if it is spreading to my knuckles on my pointer finger. I was nervous and ready to go to the emergency room even though it was late again and I was not willing to take Michael out at night. I called my best friend Jay to see if he could watch Michael at my house while I went to the emergency room. Like most of the time, he's able to watch him and he will without a question. I'm thankful God placed a friend like him in my life. If I was never a part of Dream Trips I would not have known him until who knows.

When he arrived at my house, I got into the car and was about six minutes away from Carolinas Medical Center Main (CMC). When I got to CMC Main the wait time was not long. I was able to see the doctor within 30 minutes. I explain to him everything that is going on and how I went to urgent care earlier, the pills they prescribed for me, instructions that were given and that I had followed but now my hand was hurting even more. The doctor ordered a x-ray for my hand to make sure damage had not been done to my bones, tissues or other damages. I didn't know that cellulitis was very serious infection that could cause damage to the nerves in my hand and spread through my bloodstream. The nurse put me on an IV drip and gave me pain medicine. After the doctor assessed all platforms he told me to give the medicine some time and take some Tylenol for the pain. I kept the same prescription the doctor gave me earlier when I went to urgent care. Listening to the doctors instructions going back home and having faith trusting the process. The next day came I was taking the pills on time but every time I would take them after a few hours it would be painful. Against Tylenol pills, pain medicine to be honest all pharmaceutical drugs because not natural so I do not consent in my body unless the pain is uncontrollable. At this present time the way I felt was in the category of **unbearable pain**. I was taking pain medicine to relieve the pain. My hand was still swollen and sensitive to the touch. Having a super active four your old boy in the house, pain and a disabled hand that I do everything was definitely a challenge to my parenting and peace.

I just wanted to lie in the bed all day until it got better as the weather was still gloomy, rainy and wet. After three days passed, the area where my cellulitis started seemed to spread now towards my knuckles because they were swelling even more. This particular time I was unable to close my hand to make a fist or bend my first three fingers. Not understanding but trusting the process of what the doctors told me. On the fourth day I started to notice a red line on my forearm starting at my thumb and going down my arm. My forearm and hand was becoming itchy and I found myself unaware of me scratching my arm. I went to my neighbor's house to use a phone charger because my charger was no longer working. I recall sitting on the couch using my phone to google the medicine, Cetaphil, that I was taking and the condition I had. Something I usually participate in because they need to know that what is going with my body is important to me. And particularly when reading the symptoms of the medicine I was taking, it said if you have allergic reactions such as: itchiness, redness etc. I got my phone and my neighbor gave me his charger now to have, I was having an allergic reaction to the medication. I thought *'how can this be, 'with me never having been allergic to anything in 23 years of my life'*. I grabbed Michael and rushed to a different emergency room facility on the other side of town CMC University; thinking this entire time how I was most likely sabotaging myself not getting better.

When we arrived and signed in, the wait time was short and less than 40 minutes. When I was booked into the room, the nurse came in as I explained to her my symptoms, what I was enduring, for how long and the third time in the ER not getting better with my diagnosis of the allergic reaction. The doctor came assessed the problem agreed with my original theory of being allergic to the medicine they hooked up to my IV drip with antibiotics as well as putting me on steroids to reduce swelling and gave me Tylenol for pain. They watched me for two hours in the room coming to check on me to see how I was doing. They noticed the swelling going down. The pain was subsiding and the redness was disappearing. To make sure it did not spread down infecting a major vein that could lead to a more serious problem. Michael was his happy self, playful... eating graham crackers and watching TV lying in the hospital bed beside me. I did not have to remove him from the bed to the chair because he did not want to lie still beside me. I was happy that he was his normal self. I embraced the moment instead of being frustrated. It was such a blessing to see him dancing and being silly. I felt so much better after the antibiotics were finished, my hand actually decrease in size due to all the medications. When the doctor came back in to review results before discharging me, she did come to the determination of me having an allergic reaction to the medicine. At that moment and 23 years old, I have found my first allergy. As a child to teen my mom kept me in good health with good foods and exercise.

She never wanted certain health issues we suffered from as a family to affect me and my brother. I was never sick or had any bites outside of mosquitoes growing up. My first time ever experiencing a serious issue was 18, when I was at my mom's house staying between houses. I caught scabies. Never having any health problems led me to be disgusted and in disbelief. My hand was my next tragic experience, unknowingly appearing in my journey of life. Finally the next couple of days my hand got better. My skin on my hand was peeling from where the start of the cellulitis began. Now this was Friday that I left the ER for my cellulitis. No more than four days later I was in the emergency room for detached retina. Then from surgery to bed rest for a week and one more steroid medication. All I can say is... but God.

Things could have been worse and I know God makes no mistakes.

Again, hear me clearly… God makes no mistakes. Every part of your journey as you are choosing to walk with Christ is no mistake. If you are at a place in life where questions arise questioning your life even when things are saying there are not so appealing hold on to God's word so you can continue to experience great Access. Lean not to your understanding but trust God and understanding. On your journey of life as you review look to see how that time of struggle lead you to your next big move or miracle God had destined for you. The first step chases say for journey of life is to understand you have access no matter what your circumstances. Each moment in your life is a scene in a movie the only difference is we cannot pause, take five, nor do it over. It is happening now you have to go to eat but God gave us a choice on this journey called life. God gave us the choice to do it with him or we can reject him and do it by ourselves. Choosing God is the only way. Believing in him makes the process of your journey a lot more peaceful. Never telling you it would be easier but it will be more peaceful and worth it. Any trials come keep going, breath trusting God Access, live your best life, laugh while doing it, love unconditionally and enjoy the journey as you are going towards the handpicked reality you want to live. It is coming to pass. The Lord said…' *ask and you shall receive*'. Remember he never tells you when until it come. Patience and faith in the process allows you to stay encourage as you continue your journey designated for you. As you know where you want to go, because you have plan, you wrote it out. You move towards the goal you wrote out no matter the road stumps in your journey knowing with Christ you have full access. Stay on the road to the handpick reality you created as you allow God to guide your journey through the spirit. I could have canceled myself out after each trial not pushing towards my visions of my reality; being numb to each circumstance giving up. Instead every experience I went through I look back to say thank you Lord it had to happen this way. Writing this book to you would have not come in this order format. Ironically the first time I pick the pen up in the Melbourne Hotel it was not as clear as it is now on how to structure what I wanted to write about other than God's word. He took me through to have a powerful testimony to share with his word. To inform you on your journey you have access to God to get you through. During this season of my journey and any trials I have experience I found, learned more about myself. You will see your strength, courage and cool do you want to become. Finding who you are is important to God doing your life so you can complete the desires in your heart. Not what anyone else says you are but what God says who he created you to be. With his word and understand the access he gives through his son Jesus Christ will help guide you in determining who he created you to be. He set your pathways when you trust him. Your journey being complicated understand you have a big God as you go through it that takes care of big problems, no matter how it looks stay focused on your design purpose for your dream journey climbing through the stairs to reach the top of the mountain.

CHAPTER 6
THE PROCESS

GOD'S WORD IS TRUE INDEED TO whomever believes shall endure his grace. Understanding the access got grants is because we believe in the resurrection of his son Jesus Christ is far greater than any understanding of what you can do for yourself. The journey of your life is already playing the way it is supposed to go. When you have certain experiences that are not appealing to you most likely God ordained it. All of the time we want to consider everything wrong or bad that happens in our live is the *'enemy Satan or the devil'* but once he grabs the understanding that God will never allow the enemy to hurt us or hinder us without God having a say it becomes easier to deal with the circumstances. Every time something bad happens most identify as anything but God having something to do with the bad. But I'm here to tell you that will not be the case if you believe in him. Fully believe in God allows you to eliminate doubt that you are not being taken care of. God knows the unseen, meaning what we possibly see as bad it could undeniable be worse that could have happened that we do not know about. I used to get so upset when things did not go as planned for me or "bad "had happened unexpected doing the plans I had. During those times of me getting upset looking back I was not trusting God fully. Questioning why did this happen. It was not supposed to happen like this. My plans always mess up. Screaming God why? Not understanding the full access that we have through Jesus Christ.

Really accepting that god has my best interest. One particular day I was on Facebook I seen a post. It was about a man talking to God about how can He allow bad things to happen to him that day. The man started his day behind schedule because he woke up late, his truck took hours to start and during lunch time, he had to wait longer because the food served to him was not right. But then, God replied with all of the reasons why. He said that the man woke up late that day because His angel is fighting off the demon who was beside the man in his sleep. There was an accident about to happen when the person was trying to start his car and most of all, the person who was preparing the man's lunch was having colds and God won't allow the man to catch it. You see, everything has a reason. Just learn how to trust God and never doubt that His plan is always better than our plan. This day change my entire life. I knew what it look like to completely trust the God now. My perspective shifted feeling so ungrateful before for getting upset with how my experiences on my journey was coming about from this moment up until now I walk confidentially in life with any twist that does not go as my plan because I believe my father in heaven will never for sake me only have my best interest because I am his child. God loves us more than our fleshly earthly parents do. My advice is truly except his word, obey his word and believe in him. God has a better interest in your life will be and then you do for yourself. Trust the one who knew your parents before they thought of you. It can be easily discouraging and overwhelming when our plans go opposite than what is expected. That is the plan of the enemy to have you discovered so you can lose faith, not trust in God, and begin to play mind tricks on you that will open the door giving him access to detour your defined purpose. When the plans in our life journey takes a different role still jump, shout and rejoice with joy as if those were the exact plans you created.

In your subconscious mind knowing that God will never plan something different if it was not greater for His glory and better for your purpose. Move intentionally and rejoicing for His plans are your plans no matter what plans you had written. For it is written that God will give you the promises of your heart. You can trust that he will because he created and put those desires of the promises in your heart to have. If you were to ever consider to question ask why? Ask yourself why would God give me desired that would not be fulfilled That he gave to me placing in my heart ? Now the answer to that question will always be he will not. Understand

God even as His word says He will always give you the desires placed in your heart. It will not always be according to your time when it comes to pass but the word says it shall come to pass. As believers knowing the access we hold through Christ, we hold on to knowing that "it shall come to pass." Recall a time when you ask your parents to take you to your favorite place and they said yes you can go but not right now because of work, other extra activities, or bad timing but the answer was still yes. Then on one unexpected day your parents say come on let's go or you pulling up without acknowledgment to the location you asked to go some time ago. During the time frame you could have started to become discouraged that your parents was not going to take you where you asked to go or you asked to do but surprisingly they did not forget. In relation God does the same He will never forget about you and your needs or desires you ask for. It's all about having faith knowing who you serve. Trusting in his timing for what we asked for. When we trust God timing we will not be discouraged, fearful or worried. That means as we begin tonight see things manifest when and how we expect when we ask for what our hearts desires. We still continue to have hope in our heart with knowing intentionally the Lord has everything we need. Patient is way of life virtue to everlasting greatness especially being a part of the kingdom of God. Rushing God timing is no such thing, if you beginning to do things without

God you will have now turn into your own timing, your own way of doing what you desire. Which of course God gives us free will to make that choice on our own? It is up to you fully on the route you would like to go. Your way might not be as enjoyable or have some hiccups in the road you would not have to endure because you rush where God does not have you ready for. The reason it is best to allow God to work on His time and for us to choose to allow Him to fully work on His time so we can endure the promises not missing what He has for you. Sometimes more than often we are not mentally, physically or emotionally ready for what the plans God has prepared for us. God takes his time with each of his children giving him the ability to take us and mold us so we don't lose it, take for granted the places, things or people he blessed us with. God will always be ready to meet us where we left him. When we rush our life the way we think it supposed to go we are basically telling God we don't need him or trust him. We are basically leaving him to do "our thing "as if we know the plans we have is best. Just as if you were back home with your parents or guardian and they tell you not yet the time is not now but you find away to do it anyway because you believe you are ready. As time goes on your parents no longer getting in your way, they let you go letting you experience for yourself the journey, thinking or desire you rush for. You will endure everything that comes with not being patient, moving your own speed, and not trusting the process. Yes you can still get to the goal but indeed process would be different. When we begin to understand how the access God gives us is the foundation to acquiring everything that we can possibly have obtained and develop. Our guard of defense or having control hinders the access is that we are supposed to have through Christ. As an adult imagine you have been praying for a promotion but someone else gets the promotion before you and you have been working long hours, coming in early, picking up extra shifts, over delivering to your boss, going above and beyond with clients, getting your team sales up, leading the team without being asked, turning in work before deadline or due date, leading with integrity, working the hardest for the promotion available losing sleep throughout the day, bringing your boss coffee or lunch, but now you are say upset with the boss for not choosing you. Asking yourself why I not received a promotion over your coworker. Telling yourself how you should have done things different. Beating yourself up about how far you went and still not get notice for the position. Don't cry because you feel betrayed. With God asking him "why ", why did you not get promotion. (Which is considered now an insult; hurting God not trusting his decisions.) As you are now beating yourself up about the miss felt opportunity as maybe days months or years passed your boss calls you in their office to tell you that they notice all the great work effort you have been working wanted to offer you a higher position over the one you originally desired for.

You excited jumping inside you except the offer now walking out head high your dogs are racing "you did it. "Now in this moment you experiencing that "you did it and realizing that God has already multiplied your expectations as you thought Your boss, god and all your hard work failed you for the promotion god was preparing a table / plan for his purpose Greater than what you hope for at that moment of your handpick life. Next month you understand that God has his purpose of your life in your best interest you and fully trust him with the desires of your heart and where we are supposed to be. Without complaining, blaming, or any feelings of discouragement only feelings of gratitude and mercy that God has all the timing align with your handpicked life. This allows the process to be moved by God to you. I cannot emphasize enough how allowing God to move in your journey the process will be rewarding through your trials. As you write, plan go through with the process living, loving, laughing and keep pushing that God will see you through for all the desires of your heart.. You have to be in alignment with him having full control.

I understand we like having expectations on everything that is done or happened to us. From places, people, and things we have expectations and anticipating things. Depending on the background is typically makes what type of expectation toward what goes on through our life or to our life. Take a moment and clear out every expectation you have on everything in life other than trusting God has you best. Clear out your mind your expectations of relationships, Experiences, friendships, parenting, working, cooking, and everything else that has your expectations and put that expectation in it. When you decide to stand on the solid rock that God is your expectation has no room because God is the great I am gives us the order to never give up hope. I.e. expect to anything other than himself and his word. Our expectations will fail us but more so it will give us an experience that we possible miss because we expected more from it than what we received but what we miss that matter the most to God for us to grasp to make the best new experience during the process of our life.

When you lack expectations you want your results but it's only in Gods results we reach our fullest destiny. Expecting anything from anyone other than knowing that word is true causing you to have emotions i.e. feelings. That's why it is best to put no trust in any moment other than in God. He is the solid rock foundation which will never have your feeling hid in dismay. He is the Great I AM through which you have access. He has your best interest which cause you under any situation to know that whatever the outcome happens to be, no matter how it looks there it is what it is supposed to be because you know who you obey, follow, listen and allow them to guide you up until that moment God. He knew before you knew the moment you are in. God grace got and kept you during that moment. If you trust him you will obey his word, standing on his solid rock foundation. Standing on his solid rock foundation allows you to be strong and of courage when the storm comes.

Nothing is so strong or too big for God to handle. As you are standing on his rock(being still) not discouraged, not fearful, not worried, not dismayed, not irrational, God is working in your life, providing, protecting as the storm is coming. You notice as your mind and thoughts are only focusing on what God is capable of from what his promises tells you and that your peace of mind has not left through the winds of the storm. You can see yourself going through yet another storm but Now you're on the rock notice the difference you can feel your feet you are not numb, you can switch your hips, you can clap your hands, you can lift your head high and not down to cry. You can shout praise not hide under the covers. You can smile ear to ear knowing God is here. He is here in the moment of your storm. The storm is loud the trees are whistling through wind, hail is pouring, branches and debris is flying, a tornado is few meters out, chaos surrounding you in every area, everything looks like a battlefield shifting and moving. Last of the storm rolls away but the rock had not swayed shook or shifted. Laughing, loving, helping and serving all in the mist of the storm. Believing, trusting, and faithfulness standing on God's rock foundation.

Walking in the light through Christ, now the storm completely passed that came to break you did not even harm you because of you changing how you stand during the storm. You no longer have to be fretful when you don't have money to pay bills. You no longer have to be sad because the doctor results said cancer. You no longer seek vengeance when your child or spouse disrespects you; no longer lusting put your hopes into money, things, or others to heal your pain. You will now stand in boldness know who heals, fixes, and calms the storms. This storm is here to test your faith make you fall or even kill you but as long as you stay in God's presence you will come strong and not moved when storms come. The storm is considered to be any problems or trials that arise in your life. God wants us to not be tempted when storm comes, he wants us to call on him. No need to run, or to fight it is mandatory to go through the process. The process of your journey will make or break your destiny by how you and who you choose to stand with.

Understanding the access, you have through Christ you cannot continue to run or you will not experience the access that you have. God is in the unknown, walk by faith not by sight is a guide to enduring the access he has for you. If it looks hard for your Neighbor that is not your story you have access to Gods favor so do not assume it is hard for you as well. You walk, talk, and live in truth of Gods favor he grants all of us. Trust and speak (leads to belief) that everything is great because I have God on my side and if it is hard, expect it say "thank you God! "This is for my good! "Today is millions of Americans and billions of people across the nations of the world currently are on a at stay at home order more than 10 million people have file for unemployment, over 20,000 deaths, and no protective cure for medical professionals. In North Carolina to store soda water, food and tissue paper, close meat plants, stores, beaches, restaurants, bars schools, and parks the only thing that is allowed to be out is essential workers and those collecting essential need. Movie theaters, malls, a shopping center is no longer operating. Businesses that are able to operate from home set up their employees from home. The world is a complete uproar in a global pandemic. A virus name COVID-19, a strain of the corona virus. A plague that has changed life as we formally knew it. God has sent his wrath upon his world as stated in the word.

The world is now facing major changes. We find ourselves leaning on each other to stand in the love of God. People are not able to pay bills from being out of work for more than two months and maybe months from now. Small business is losing their business can't pay employees. Meal preps are going to homes and donated groceries. Some people waiting hours in line and at drive-through buying poultry by pounds from Case markets. Only COVID-19 or ER facilities open no surgeries being performed. Wearing gloves and mask to every place. Buying Lysol and making hand sanitizer. Stocks are lowest in history. Social distancing is the new form of living. 6 feet distance, no touch, No contacts.

Nursing homes are shutting down. Navy ships are on pause. Thousands of unclaimed bodies buried on top and made a grave in New York on top of each other. Family is dying insects. Hospitals cannot have visitors to any patients. Churches are close now online streaming. Pastors and priests are just around the world. No one never imagining that the world will look the way it is. During these times the best thing to do is trust the process. Do not be faint to the media and have faith in God. Know you have the favor of the Lord to be not worried. God want us to pray to him when we get distracted easy comes to correct. To his children who believe we are covered from his wrath. Changing the lens of perspective during these unprecedented times and the new norm to come is very important. you can see it as the dark cane to steal the light due to the economic crash and the unfortunate lives lost or the light that came took its course bringing unity between nations, politicians and small businesses working together, families spending quality time, communities and neighbors impacting medical fields by giving back, and realizing non violent inmates home early, gas is affordable the lowest in decades, bills are paused, government sent economic impact checks out, surfaces are becoming cleaner and the ozone layer is back to normal.

Air pollution is great, crime rates across the nation down, more people coming together loving thy neighbor than before. Depending on the lens of perspective prepares your outcome during these moments. Currently the Covid 19 Pandemic shows us nothing under the sun what we thought we did in our day-to-day lives matter does not. At this moment you are able to show the access you have through Christ because you choose to believe in him. Now being Able to walk in the authority during your process of your journey obeying Gods word. So many blessings and answered prayers are through the times of hardship or change. In your lens you see it as a setback but God sent it as a fuel jet pack. Stay connected to hearing God speak to you in every area of your life. If you cannot understand the voice of God you will have difficult time knowing the direction he wants you to go.

Learning to hear the voice of God and the Holy Spirit comes from reading the holy bible, applying Gods word and commandments to become clearer to your spirit, praying for wisdom to be wise to his voice not yours and following the Holy Spirit, forgive others and repent to God daily for your sins, becoming more like of Christ, and allowing Christ to live within you without a fight of changing the you, you once knew. Becoming one with God and the Holy Spirit requires you to become *"born"* again. When you first accept Jesus Christ as your savior you are considered saved received the Holy Ghost and you are growing in the speaking in language. Receiving a water baptism is the sign and choice you made to declare to God you are ready to walk in his way surrender all your ways to him now a new you born again with the Holy Spirit.

The Holy Spirit give you insight direction, on your choices best to make, He is the thing that you feel in the moment of decision making even if it do not look like this is what others would do it has you wanting to pursue because God through the Holy Spirit is using you as the vessel. Choose the spirit decision that brings you peace. I never intentionally come from a place of hurt despair the more you choose from the spirit from inside of you that is from God you will hear and walk the map to your destiny. Your feelings of certainty knowing who God is, who you are through Christ, who called you to be in his kingdom, you are an authentic witness of The testimonies of his work in your life, who is son of God Jesus Christ, where God stands in your heart, God word will not go void, there is no other God but the one and only one that we worship and praise, God gives you life and breath and, God gives you full access in power to spread the light in the world while living in full authority in his name. God can do magnificent things that no one else can do in our personal and love when lives. The prices on your journey to your destiny are special… embrace every moment. The road might not be easy but God will never turn his back on you. He did not bring you this far to leave you no matter where you are currently at in your process on your journey, you are able to be reading this book or receiving this message.

God saying don't give up now it might not look like what you expect, I know you're tired, I know you're hurt, I know you feel alone, I know you have not prayed in a while, I know your business not succeeding right now, I know your health evaluation, but I am here. Cast your cares upon the Lord he will take care of your needs. Always remain moving towards your goal, keep your heart and ears open for God to move in your life, do not try to understand the logic *"why"* God does but instead continue to allow the Holy Spirit to lead guide your steps. It's all worth it through your journey will look back from time to time recognizing the evidence of God and what he could do through you.

CHAPTER 7
BE U. BE BEAUTIFUL.
BE DIFFERENT

G OD CREATED YOU AND NO OTHER individual exactly like you. As you were in your mother's womb before you became an embryo God had the specialty qualities of who he created you to be. The gifts and the desires of your heart a place before your first breath. It is in that moment after our first breath your potential and the light God placed is shown throughout. You begin to have options and choices to choose from. Becoming more of the inner you, learning more of the qualities that you have as you are growing. Separating the things places or people in different categories of your satisfaction.

Tapping into everything you want surrounded by you. God gift to God is you doing what you are good at. Be yoU. Sometimes as humans often you can have thoughts of what you are suppose be doing with your life. Or what does God have plan for me? Understanding God has equipped you through your natural skills and talent abilities to fulfill your purpose. If you are not sure of the purpose of your journey, do what you are good at and you will see everything God has for you will be blessed by him. Without noticing no matter what your talents are you gain great pleasure when you do what you are naturally phenomenal at doing. You will feel God's presence on the work you put towards the project. Operating in your natural talent glorifies God and manifest life for others. Talents from God are identifiable because they come without application of force. Can you recall a time you went through a food stop and the server was miserable at doing her job? Well the server works in a job where they are not gifted at. When you are in your proper place you will excel in the jobs and be a blessing (asset) to your employers and those you're working around. You will blossom in your gift and show God's light through your work and considering God created all of us differently he speaks to you through his anointing power. Gave to you at birth joy and peace. When God places your gift inside of you when you are in your mom's womb it will remain inside of you until God takes you home. Be confident as you operate in your gift during the journey. If you can stand in your talent that God's grace you with and move with selfless intent trusting God he will continue to add fruit and multiply. God needs us as he strategically placed and purposely created each of us to our own personal distinctness.

God knew conditions, circumstances, parents, place, living conditions, surroundings and our flesh hearts would not be equal among the nations to ever feel discouraged or down by not operating the same when God is using it for the works of the nations but God gives you the choice to choose to be you. Jealousy or envy idolatry is a scheme of the enemy; the devil wants you to not operate in your gift and focus on how you can be better at someone else's. It allows your journey to be led forcefully of unwanted trials and errors. God wants you to be rooted in place; we were not always God people. You were adopted into the royal family of God's kingdom. God wants to make sure he always has a personal relationship with you.

When God deals with each of us, he deals with us individually as a father to his child. Nothing other than you matters to God when he is encountering you. God is proud to be a father to his children. He loves having your attention to himself so you can exercise and have the wisdom to see the provision of your life. No one can change God's mind about who you are not even yourself. He created and gave order to who you are to be on earth. It is up to you only to tap into who he called you to be. No one can look at your life as long as you have access through Christ and talk down about your circumstances. Jesus was in Nazareth and everyone heard that the "carpenter" was the son of God I.e. the chosen one who God sent to heal the land they did not believe that Jesus is who he said he is. Jesus is so special, the one and only man of God and so many people, unbelievers that were around Jesus that did not want to believe in him and the power gifts he has inside of him. Those unbelievers choose not to believe Jesus because he was just a carpenter. He looked unworthy to them because of his "earthly title and appearance." These unbelievers did not have faith they only believed in and trusted the things that lacked faith in Jesus. They missed the miracle of works that was for them.

It is very important to know that during those times Jesus knew some people who in Nazareth would not believe he continued to be the Son of God obeying his father's word of who he was called to be. He walked the earth healing faith believers, those who have the vision to see past their eyesight and that Jesus is the one and only son of God. Jesus was tempted many times to change who his father called him to be for what the earth feels is a greater reward of power and gifts which in reality would seem far more rewarding but as the saying goes "if you lose your soul to gain the world it is not worth it "and Jesus knew that. Jesus knew his purpose and mission on earth was for a season. Jesus knew unbelievers would harass him because he would be steadfast in the land from the dictators delivering people from them giving believers hope, peace, and joy through the spirit of Christ. Jesus loved those all. Jesus knew who he was with on earth no matter the ridicule he kept moving in his mission. He came here on earth form to make us understand we are one through Christ.

Love thy neighbor no materials matter in deciding who to love, be kind to, help or care for because we all are equal through Christ blood. We bleed and have the same flesh skin. Jesus being a carpenter symbolizing that you don't need clothes materials to have power. The enemy's biggest form of luring you into his trap is materials and things you want when you suppose to have them; it will come only with the price of believing in Christ obeying the commandments it comes freely and fruitfully. The enemy is Satan, who was once an angel that wanted to be like God. He wanted the same power as his creator, he did not want to obey God rules in heaven. The devil was acting of turmoil and God kicked him out of his kingdom. Now Satan recruits and tries to defeat God, but he knows he can't win. Satan's goal is to make you be far from experiencing Christ and his favor. So, Satan will do anything and everything to come between you and God.

This is the ultimate goal of his. He manipulates you into thinking what you can gain through him is far greater, better feeling, more rewarding than walking faithfully with Christ living through you. Everything you gain through the plots of the enemy is not everlasting. Galatians 6:7 (KJV) tell us what we sow we shall reap. The enemy doesn't want you to sow great things he wants you to divide, disobedient, steal, cheat, lie, be angry, mad, malicious, sarcasm, mean, murder, kill, evil for evil, no love, hatred fights, rape, assault, lack of patience, lack of kindness, abuse. Anytime you find yourself putting out these forms of actions you are going to reap what comes from it.

You will not know the day of the hour, but God will NOT be mocked. God wants us to sow loyalty, trust, honor, grateful, positive, peace, happiness, gratitude, patience, love to thy neighbor, kindness, boldness, confidence, joy, ten percent of income, caring, smiles, hugs, time, hard work, dedication, servant ship, leadership, praise of his name, worship his name, and your heart. No matter what or how you find yourselves right now you have the moment to choose from now what you will sow in your harvest. The enemy will put traps, tricks, sticks and stones to have you sow seeds from his garden as he did to Adam and Eve when they ate the apple. As he will make you feel in that moment you won because you have that "thing" he lured you in which is something you already wanted. He plays a game of deception Satan only wins with deceiving you in thinking God is not for you or that time matters.

Time in life no debate is not ours. You do not have control over time so do not try to control the events, you will try if you do not understand how to adjust to being content with peace of how time operates even possibly driving you to a place feeling scattered, unstable mentally, to be stable in everything going on time as planned. If Satan can leverage your desires for your life for his plans to turn your ways to him. Satan recruits for his army, he works hard and diligently to set up plots to deceive you in operating in your flesh not by your spirit. His plots leave you what you want so you could miss the sign of deceit. God tells us blessed is the man who endures temptation, for when he has been approved, he will receive the crown of life which the lord has promised to those who love him. " *James 1: 12 KJV* In his world it also tells us *James 1:16 KJV* do not be deceived, my beloved Brethren.

Every good gift and every perfect gift are from above and comes down from the father of lights with whom is no variableness, neither shadow of turning. Meaning everything may feel, look, smell, sound and taste like it is great but it does not come From God above it not what meant for you to have. ***Hebrews 13:5KVJ*** let your conduct be without covetousness be content with such things as you have. For he himself has said "I will never leave you nor forsake you." You can always trust the Lord's word to keep you in alignment on your journey. My favorite quote "everything that glitter is not gold." On your journey as you are going through the process you want authenticity for it is pure; the truth. You will always find light in the truth.

The lord is where the light is at. As you keep pushing, never give up, smile, endure the process being true to who God placed in your spirit and heart, you will have access to God's authority and dominion over ALL things. Embrace the BeaUty about yoU because it is no other like the yoU God created. It could be the one thing someone considered weird or no one else has but if we change the lens of view it was never meant for anyone to have that talent, gift, trait or ability. Be EXCITED. The moment where life makes sense knowingly and GRAB HOLD TO IT and you tap into yoU. God gave you AUTHORITY to do so. God gave you ACCESS to do so. God gave you HIS POWER to do so. Your parents, spouse, friends, boss, and family can NOT do anything more than what God can do for yoU. Be confident when you speak about the yoU God created yoU to be, the walk of life it takes to have his access because it's no one else like him. You are special to have God's access. Life and the world we live in today 2020 so many different outlets and ways of living and forms of life to choose. It is easy to get so hung up on just doing this a certain way and want control getting all worked up out of character that you forget to just simply live and endure the things God has for yoU to enjoy.

Always remember to repeat with me "what I want is not what I always need. God you know what's best for me and your timing is better than mine. "Pray and talk to go daily as you on your journey instead of having conversations with yourself (voices in your head) include God in them when you are talking as if he was in front of you. Get comfortable with allowing him to come in your heart as you are having a conversation with him. God loves you so much he is waiting on you. God wants you to Be beautiful, be different and most of all Be yoU on your journey.

SCRIPTURE PAGES

Below you will find scriptures that are special to me because I asked God to lead me to the message for the people that he would like for me to share specifically for his glory. I was reading my morning scriptures everyday creating a new practice for my spiritual relationship with God by praying asking God to lead me to what he wants me to know, grow and learn about him; opening the bible to where the spirit led with no intentions of the message of where I was going to be reading from. I stored them in my notes to go back to later to share through media content, when God gave me provision to put in my book as a delay of not sending an email procrastinating not listening to my spirit on urgency to put in my book. The day I decided to transfer from my phone to work on my own time God deleted it from my notes and hysterical almost because I love the vision, he shared with me to put in the book instead of originally sharing through media content. At that moment my heart paused, the history tab popped up somehow and there it was, my deleted history scripture pages. I appreciate and value the moment God showed me what it would be like not to have his words to share and these scriptures below until that moment I didn't realize how much intimacy is between me and each scripture making sure I am obedient to God in sharing them with you because it's a privilege and honor to work for the Lord kingdom

Read the full pages left to right of the scripture page, write what message you receive and facts you learn from God's word in your Axcess workbook.

- ☐ Hoel 11:1
- ☐ Psalm 72:14
- ☐ Matthew 13:14
- ☐ 1 Samuel 14:37

- [ ] John 16:3
- [ ] Deuteronomy 23:11
- [ ] Jeremiah 6:7
- [ ] Matthew 9:36
- [ ] Luke8:38
- [ ] Jeremiah 6:7 amp
- [ ] 1 Samuel 6:8
- [ ] 2 Corinthians 1
- [ ] 1 Thessalonians 2:17
- [ ] Psalm 149:4 - Proverbs 1
- [ ] 2 Chronicles 19:7
- [ ] Ezekiel 1-3:19
- [ ] Daniel8:14
- [ ] Mark 6:26
- [ ] Hebrews 9:26
- [ ] Acts 22:7
- [ ] 2 King 18:9
- [ ] Hosea 8:8
- [ ] 1 Samuel 9:1
- [ ] 1 Samuels 3:9
- [ ] Isiah 66:22-Jeremiah 1-3:8
- [ ] Acts 26:11
- [ ] Psalms 72:14
- [ ] Luke 13:24
- [ ] Deuteronomy 31:17
- [ ] 2 Samuel 24:7-1kings
- [ ] Ezekiel 48:15
- [ ] Romans 2:28
- [ ] Exodus 2:11
- [ ] Psalms 54:7
- [ ] Psalm 19:10
- [ ] genesis 1:27
- [ ] Exodus 2:11
- [ ] Jeremiah 10:25
- [ ] 1 Thessalonians 2:17
- [ ] Nehemiah 5:14

- [ ] Galatians 5-6
- [ ] Colossians 2:3
- [ ] Galatians 6:7
- [ ] Job 30:14
- [ ] John 13
- [ ] James 1:19
- [ ] Ephesians 4: 31
- [ ] Colossians 4:6

Do not forget God's word is about sharing with others so he can live through everyone. Do not try out run the pace of grace.

"AXCESS MERCHANDISE"

AXCESS MERCHANDISE
You can find online at *Uniqueworldwide.world*

ABOUT THE AUTHOR

Unique Davis was born and raised in Charlotte NC. She has been devoted to Christ since the age of four years old. Having faith and going to church she grew up as an authentic witness to the spirit of God. She is an entrepreneur owning multiple businesses located in Charlotte NC. She is very hard working, caring, loving, mother, friend, woman that helps in the community. Her faith practices have exalted her life through challenging times like losing both of her parents. Now at the age of 25 as she continues to travel , live in fullness, spread positivity, and being the light in the world her day to day joy is bringing awareness about the spirit of the lord.

Printed in the United States
by Baker & Taylor Publisher Services